Skills On
Studying

HELP IS ON
THE WAY
FOR:

Written Reports

Written by Marilyn Berry
Pictures by Bartholomew

CHILDRENS PRESS ™

CHICAGO

Childrens Press
School and Library Edition

Producers: Ron Berry and Joy Wilt Berry
Editor: Kate Dickey
Consultant: Kathy McBride
Design and Production: Abigail Johnston
Typesetting: Curt Chelin

c 2

ISBN 0-516-03234-8

So your teacher assigned a **written report!**

Hang on! Help is on the way!

If you are having a hard time

- choosing a topic,
- finding facts about a topic,
- organizing your thoughts, or
- putting your thoughts into words...

...you are not alone!

Just in case you're wondering...

...why don't we start at the beginning?

What is a Written Report?

A written report is information about a specific topic collected from different resources and set down in writing. A good written report is
- accurate
- organized
- easy to understand
- to the point
- interesting
- informative

Why Does Your Teacher Want You To Do a Written Report?

1. A written report gives you a chance to learn about something on your own and to share it with others.

2. Learning how to do a good written report will be important for your success in school.

3. Working on a written report helps you practice many important skills, such as
- reading,
- using the library,
- taking notes,
- organizing your thoughts,
- making outlines, and
- putting your thoughts in writing.

Before You Begin Working On Your Report

1. **Check the assignment.** Find out exactly what your teacher wants in your report. If there is anything you do not understand, ask questions. Be sure to find out

 how long the report should be,

 when the report is due,

 if an outline or progress reports are required, and

 • if there is a form to follow.

2. Get organized! Once you have found out the due date for your report, set up a schedule. The schedule should include a deadline for each step of your report. If you stick to your schedule, you will write a better report and avoid a last-minute panic.

WRITTEN REPORT SCHEDULE	
deadline	step
May 3	Topic approved
May 5	Informal outline
May 15	Research completed
May 17	Final outline
May 21	Rough Draft
May 24	Check Rough Draft
May 25	Take a break
May 28	Final Draft
May 30	Finishing touches
May 31	Hand in Report

3. Set up a special folder. You are going to be gathering a lot of important notes as you work on your report. It will help to keep all of your notes in one folder. You can start with your list of special instructions and your schedule.

Eight Steps to Writing a Report

There are eight simple steps to writing a good report. It's going to take some time, but it doesn't have to be difficult. The key is to work on your report a little each day and to take it **one step at a time!**

STEP 1. CHOOSE A TOPIC

Choosing your topic is a very important part of your written report. The decisions you make at this point will affect your whole report. To help yourself choose a good topic, do these things:

- **Check the assignment.** You may need to choose from a given list of topics, or your teacher may allow you to choose your own. Just make sure your choice fits the assignment.

- **Choose something interesting**. It is very important to choose a topic that is interesting to you. Try to pick something you will enjoy reading about. If you are excited about your topic, you will pass that excitement on to the reader.

Do some quick research. Once you have a topic in mind, take a quick trip to the library. Find out if there is material available on your topic at your reading level. Find out if your topic is too broad or too narrow. If there is no information on your topic, it is too narrow. If there are whole books written on your topic, it may be too broad and you may want to trim it down.

- **Get a final OK.** When you think you have chose your topic, talk with your teacher about it. It is always best to get a final OK **before** you move on to the next step.

STEP 2. MAKE AN INFORMAL OUTLINE

Once you have chosen a topic, you need to decide what you want to know about your topic. To help you decide what main points you will include in your report, you should write an informal outline.

There are two ways to choose the main points that will make up your informal outline.

1. Ask questions. Think about your topic. Make a list of questions that you would like to answer in your report.

2. Do some reading. If you do not know anything about your topic, do some reading first.
- Look up your topic in an encyclopedia.
- Try to find a children's book on your topic. Children's books often present the highlights of the subject.

These resources will give you some ideas for your informal outline.

Here are some important things to know about your informal outline:

- Your outline should include four to six questions or statements about your topic.
- When you decide on the main points of your outline, put them in a logical order and number them. You will use these numbers when you do your research.
- Form is not important. This outline is for your use only.
- Keep your outline handy when doing your research. It will keep you on track by reminding you which information is important to your report and which is not.

STEP 3. RESEARCH YOUR TOPIC

Now that you have decided on the main points of your report, it's time to start gathering information. To research your topic, you will need to
- choose your resources,
- study your resources, and
- take notes.

Choose Your Resources

The types of resources you use will depend on the topic you have chosen. A good place to start is the library. Don't be afraid to ask the librarians for help. That's part of their job.

There are three main types of resources in most libraries:

1. Reference books. These are books that contain information about many different topics. For now, you will want to read only the parts that relate to your topic. Some examples of reference books are
- encyclopedias
- dictionaries
- atlases
- almanacs
- handbooks
- bibliographies
- books in the vertical file

2. Books about your topic. You will find these books listed in the card catalog. The best place to start is the subject index. If you look closely at the cards under your topic, you will find valuable information, such as

- the title of the book,
- the length of the book,
- when the book was written, and
- what kind of information is in the book.

The information on the cards can help you choose the best books for your report.

3. Magazines, journals, and newspapers. You may find articles on your topic in magazines or journals. You can locate these articles by looking in the *Reader's Guide to Periodical Literature.* This is an especially good resource if your topic is about a current event. Newspapers can also be a valuable resource, especially for local events.

he library is not the only place to use as a source. Here is a list of other sources of formation for your report:

government agencies
personal interviews
surveys and questionnaires
films and filmstrips
television and radio
local organizations, such as businesses and museums

25

Study Your Resources

Once you have chosen your resources, it is time to study them. This is a very important part of your research. It is the time when you carefully review each of your resources and choose the information you will use in your report. To get the most out of your study time, do these thing

- Study one resource at a time. Get all the information you can. Then move on to your n resource.
- Don't read whole books. Look up your topic i the table of contents or the index, and read or the parts you can use in your report.

- Keep your informal outline handy! It will remind you of what you are supposed to be studying.

- Make sure your resources will be there when you need them. This may take some planning ahead. Try to reserve or check out books ahead of time.
- Study alone.

Take Notes

You will be gathering information from several different sources. To keep it all straight, you will need to take notes.

Using note cards. A popular and easy system of taking notes is to use 3'' x 5'' or 4'' x 6'' index cards. Using these cards will help you organize your notes for your final outline. Each note card you write should contain

- only one complete fact, idea, or quote,
- where you found the information (if it is a published source, include the title and author o the work and the page number), and
- the number of the main point under which you will include this information in your report (che your informal outline).

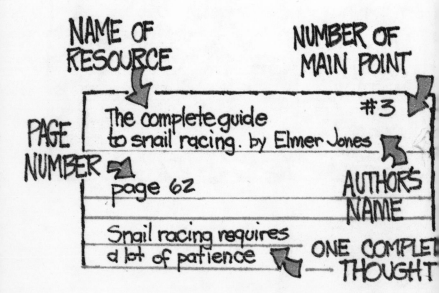

Using your own words. Most of the time you will want to put the information you find into your own words. Try this easy method:

- Read the material all the way through.
- When you come across important information, mark the place with a paper clip.
- Go through the material a second time. Review your informal outline to make sure you can use the information you have marked.
- If you can use the information, reread it and summarize it in your own words on a note card.

Using another person's words. Sometimes you will want to use another person's words, ideas, or research. Be sure to copy this information very carefully onto your note card. Put quotation marks around the words to remind you that they are not your own. If you use these words in your report, you will need to credit the person who said them or wrote them.

THAT'S A GOOD QUOTE. I'LL USE THIS.

Here are some tips to keep in mind when taking notes:
- Use only one side of the card.
- Keep your notes neat and brief.
- Try not to write down the same information tw.
- Go over your notes before moving on to anothe resource. Make sure you understand everything you have written down. Be sure you have copie quotations exactly.

Make Bibliography Cards

You will need to include in your report a list of all the resources you have used. A list of printed resources is called a **bibliography**. To be sure this list is complete, make out a card for each resource as you use it. If you use the proper form now, preparing the bibliography page for your report will be easy. Here are some examples:

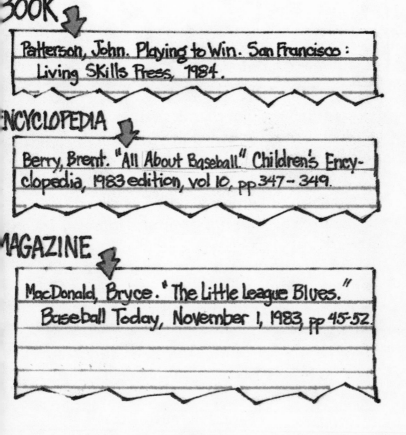

BOOK

> Patterson, John. Playing to Win. San Francisco : Living Skills Press, 1984.

ENCYCLOPEDIA

> Berry, Brent. "All About Baseball." Children's Encyclopedia, 1983 edition, vol 10, pp 347 - 349.

MAGAZINE

> MacDonald, Bryce. "The Little League Blues." Baseball Today, November 1, 1983, pp 45-52.

STEP 4. MAKE A FORMAL OUTLINE

Now that you have gathered all the information you need, it's time to organize it. A good way to organize information is to put it into a formal outline.

This outline is like a master plan that will guide you as you write your report. It will help you do the following:

- Finalize the main points of your report.
- Organize the supporting information for each of the main points.
- Make final choices as to which information you will use and which you will not.
- Stay on track by putting all your notes in a logical order.
- Save time. You can make changes and correct mistakes more easily in an outline than in a written report.

Decide on Your Theme

Part of making a formal outline is to decide on the overall theme of your report. Every bit of information in your report will relate in some way to this theme. The theme is the main idea of your report. It gives the reader a preview of what your report is about. It should be stated in one sentence, or two at the most.

Organize Your Note Cards

Before you write out your outline, you will need to organize your note cards. Start by sorting your note cards into stacks. There should be one stack for each main point of your report.

- Lay out all the cards in the first stack.
- Read the cards and think about the information. Pretend that you are trying to explain this point to someone. In what order would you reveal the information?
- Arrange the note cards in a logical order. When you are pleased with the order, number the cards and put a rubber band around them. It will help you keep the cards in order.

Do this with each stack of cards.

Write Out Your Formal Outline

To write out your formal outline, you will need your note cards, a piece of paper and a pencil.

At the top of the paper, write the title of your report.

Under the title, write the theme of your report.

Go through your note cards one by one and start writing out your outline. Each card should have a place in the outline. Discard any note card that does not.

Here is how your outline might look:

TITLE

THEME _____

1. First Main Point
   A. Sub-Point
      1. Example
      2. Example
   B. Sub-point
2. Second Main Point
   A. Sub-point
   B. Sub-point
   C. Sub-point
3. Third Main Point
   A. Sub-point
      1. Example

STEP 5. WRITE THE ROUGH DRAFT

It would be difficult to write your report perfectly on the first try. That is the reason for the rough draft. It gives you a chance to make changes and to refine your report. You will get the most out of your rough draft if you remember the following:

- Use pencils.
- Write on only one side of the paper.
- Leave space for corrections.
- Don't worry at this point about spelling, punctuation, grammar or neatness. Instead, thi about what you are trying to say.

There will be three main parts to your report. It's best to include them all in your rough draft.

1. Introduction. Here you present the theme and briefly mention the main points that will be discussed in the report.

2. Body. Here you present all the information that you have collected about your topic. It should include every point and sub-point in your formal outline.

3. Conclusion. This is a brief summary of the information given in the report. It includes a reworded version of the theme and the main points of the report. Here you may also draw your own conclusions and state your own opinions.

To write your rough draft, simply pull together all the information on your note cards.

Remember:
- Keep your outline in front of you and stick to it.
- Work on one main point of your outline at a time.
- Go through your note cards one by one and explain each piece of information as you go.

f you followed your schedule, you should have
t least one day for a break from your report.
Take it! It is always best to start your final draft
with a fresh outlook. Take this time to gather a
ew reference books that will help you with your
inal draft, such as
• a dictionary for spelling and definitions,
• a thesaurus for word selection, and
  a book on grammar.

STEP 6. REVIEW THE ROUGH DRAFT

It's a good idea to read through your report three times and make the changes as you go.

1. Check for content. Does it all relate to the theme? Are all the important points covered? Does it follow the outline? Is it accurate?

2. Check for style. Is the writing smooth? Is it to the point? Is it easy to understand?

3. Check for spelling, punctuation, and grammar. Don't forget to use your reference books.

If you can, have someone else read your report. You might try reading the report aloud. This can uncover problems you didn't see before.

Now is the time to make sure you have properly credited any person whose words, ideas, or research you have borrowed. You can do this easily in the body of your report.

If you are borrowing someone's words, follow the quote with the person's last name. If you found the words in printed material, include the year the material was published and the page number.

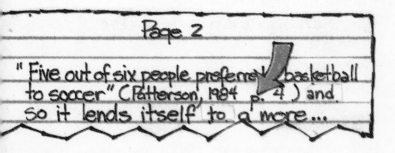

Page 2

" Five out of six people preferred basketball to soccer" (Patterson, 1984 p. 4) and so it lends itself to a more ...

You must also give credit when you are borrowing the results of another person's research.

Page 3

In a study it was found that basketball was more popular than soccer (Patterson, 1984) Leaving soccer to be kicked down into fourth place in the ...

STEP 7. WRITE THE FINAL DRAFT

At last it is time to write the final draft. The hardest part of your report is over, but don't let down yet. A report that is written neatly will show off all your hard work.

- Use black or dark blue ink, or type if you know how.
- Write on only one side of the paper.
- Leave margins on all sides.
- If your teacher has requested a special form, follow it.
- Write or type carefully.
- Watch for errors in spelling and punctuation.
- Put your last name and a page number at the top of each page.
- Proofread each page. Make corrections neatly. If there are more than three mistakes, copy the page over.

IF IT WEREN'T FOR THE SMUDGES AND PIZZA STAINS, THIS WOULD'VE BEEN AN **A** REPORT.

SIGH

STEP 8. ADD THE FINAL TOUCHES

To complete your report, you will need to add three simple pages: a title page, a table of contents, and bibliography page.

1. The title page includes the title of your report, your name, the date, and your teacher's name.

How to Write a Report
by Marilyn Berry
April 14, 1984
for
Mrs. Picayune

2. The table of contents lists the main parts of the report and their page numbers. It should list the introduction, the main points of the report, the conclusion, and the bibliography.

Table of Contents

3. The bibliography page is a list of all the sources you used in your report. Preparing this page will be easy if you made out bibliography cards and kept track of all the other resources you used.

- Put your stack of bibliography cards into alphabetical order according to the author's last name.
- Copy the information onto the bibliography pa

Your Name   Page 14

Bibliography

Berry, Brent. "All About Baseball." Children's
    Encyclopedia, 1983, vol. 10.

MacDonald, Bryce. "The Little League Blues."
    Baseball Today, Nov. 1, 1983.

Patterson, John. Playing to Win. San Fran-
    cisco: Living Skills Press, 1984.

Other Resources

Baseball Hall of Fame, Cooperstown, NY

Finally it is time to assemble your report. Put it together in this order:
Title page
Table of contents
Introduction
Body of the report (make sure the pages are in order)
Conclusion
Bibliography

Put your report in an attractive folder. You may buy one or make your own.

WARNING!

If you follow the steps in this book, you will probably write a great report, and in fact. . .

. . .you might even enjoy it!

THE END

About the Author
Marilyn Berry has a master's degree in education with a specialization in reading. She is on the staff as a producer and creator of supplementary materials at the Institute of Living Skills. Marilyn is a published author of books and composer of music for children. She is the mother of two sons, John and Brent.